Paul Revere

A Biography Funbook™

By Carole Marsh

Published by GALL**O**PADE INTERNATIONAL member and supporter of:

American Booksellers Association
American Library Association
International Reading Association
National Association for Gifted Children
The National School Supply and Equipment Association
The National Council for the Social Studies
Museum Store Association
Association of Partners for Public Lands
Association of Booksellers for Children

A Word From the Author!

Paul Revere is a popular patriot in American history. Not only famous for his help with the American Revolution, he is also known for his great skill as a gold and silversmith. This "jack of all trades" is an interesting piece of American history!

Carole Marsh

About the Author...

Carole Marsh is the creator of the Biography Funbook™ Series and author of many books on History, Geography, and Biography. She is also the creator of The 50 State Experience Series, which includes books, workbooks, software, stickers, maps, and other products for all 50 States and Canada. In 2007, she was named Georgia Author of the Year. You can write to her at fanclub@gallopade.com.

Paul Revere

Midnight Messenger

Paul was the second of at least 9 (and possibly as many as 12!) children. He was the oldest surviving son.

Paul Revere was born sometime in December of 1734. He was the son of Apollos Rivoire, a French Protestant immigrant, and Deborah Hichborn, the daughter of a local artisan family. Paul's father gradually changed his name from Apollos to Paul and from Rivoire to Revere.

Paul was born in the capital city of Massachusetts. What city is this? Circle the correct answer.

Philadelphia

Boston

Los Angeles

Paul's father came to Massachusetts from France in search of religious freedom.

Young Paul went to school at the North Writing School in Boston. He was an apprentice to his father, where he learned the art of gold and silversmithing. Paul's father died shortly before his apprenticeship was finished.

Color the tureen.

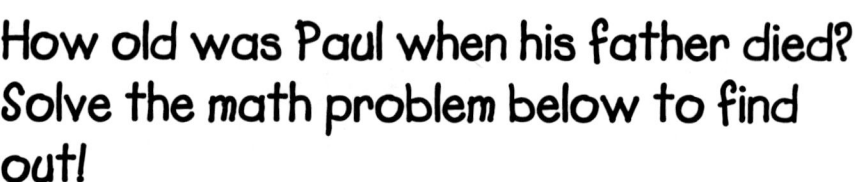

How old was Paul when his father died? Solve the math problem below to find out!

$$3 + 5 - 1 + 6 - 4 + 7 + 3$$

Paul was _____ years old.

Once his father died, Paul became responsible for his family.

In 1756, Paul served in the colonial artillery for a short time. After an unsuccessful expedition against the French, Paul returned to Boston. A few months after his return, he married Sarah Orne, often called "Sary."

Color the wedding bells.

Paul married Sarah in August of 1757. Solve the math problem below to find out how old he was!

$$1757 \text{ (year married)}$$
$$- 1734 \text{ (year born)}$$
$$\overline{} \text{ (age at marriage)}$$

Paul and Sarah went on to have 8 children!

Paul became well known as a silversmith/goldsmith, a profession he kept for over 40 years. He and his employees made many items out of gold and silver. His work was highly praised during his lifetime.

Unscramble the sentence below to find out some items Paul made.

Paul and his _____ made everything
SWOKRER

from simple _____ to
OPOSNS

beautiful _____ _____.
EAT   ETSS

Revereware is a type of kitchenware still sold today!

Paul also did other jobs when times got tough and the silversmith business was slow. Shortly before the Revolution, he began to work as a copper plate engraver. He also made illustrations for books and magazines.

The words in the sentence below are all crammed together! "Pull" them apart to find an interesting fact about Paul the dentist!

PAULOFTENCARVEDFALSETEETHFROMWALRUSTUSKS!

_____

_____!

Contrary to myth, Paul never made George Washington's false teeth!

Paul tried out the dentistry profession for a few years! He not only cleaned teeth, he also made false teeth!

Paul became active in politics through his connections with members of local groups and his friends in business. In the year before the Revolution, Paul watched and reported on the activities of British soldiers. He also was a courier (messenger) for the local patriot groups from 1770 to 1773.

Find the words in the Word Find.

Paul became a leader of the Sons of Liberty and took part in the Boston Tea Party to protest British taxation.

TEA   TAXES   BRITISH

B	L	C	V	H
R	I	N	O	Z
I	B	T	A	X
T	E	A	E	H
I	R	E	I	R
S	T	D	M	G
H	Y	R	B	E
T	O	I	R	T

Color the tea.

Paul's wife, Sarah, died in 1773. He soon remarried a woman named Rachel Walker. They had 8 more children!

In April of 1775, Paul made his famous midnight ride. Hearing that British General Gage planned to take his troops to arrest patriots John Hancock and Samuel Adams, Paul was told to warn them. He and two other men set off for Lexington and then Concord, each going a different route in case they were caught.

The other two riders were William Dawes and Dr. Samuel Prescott.

PATRIOT   COURIER   LIBERTY

C	T	M	H	P
A	D	O	J	K
E	S	B	E	C
X	G	M	B	O
U	O	C	W	H
F	V	H	G	E
D	S	I	T	S
A	P	W	C	A

The British were also planning to steal the patriots' military supplies stored at Concord.

Before leaving Boston, Paul set up a "signal" in case he was late. The "signal" was a lantern hung in the bell-tower of Christ Church. One lantern was to be hung if the British were coming by land, two were to be hung if the British were coming by water. He then crossed the Charles River to Charlestown where he borrowed a horse for his journey to Lexington.

To find out the warning Paul gave, solve the code below.

A	B	C	D	E	F	G	H	I	J	K	L	M
✹	❀	✣	♣	➤	♥	❗	✳	✂	©	☛	✈	✉

N	O	P	Q	R	S	T	U	V	W	X	Y	Z
❀	☆	◆	✡	✎	♥	☎	◗→	✚	✖	✍	✠	✓

" __ __ __ __ __ __ __ __ __ __ __
   T H E R E G U L A R S

__ __ __
A R E

__ __ __ __ __ __ !"
C O M I N G

After warning Hancock and Adams, Paul met up with William Dawes. The two men took off to warn Concord that the British Regulars were coming. They were joined on the way by Dr. Prescott. All three men were caught by the British, but Dawes and Prescott managed to escape.

Dr. Prescott finally reached Concord and alerted them of the British Regulars' plan to raid their stores of ammunition.

Put an F by the FACTS, and an O by the OPINIONS.

_____ Paul Revere was a silversmith.

_____ Paul was a brave man.

_____ Paul had a tough job as a patriot.

_____ Paul warned that the British Regulars were coming.

After being threatened and questioned by the British, Paul was released. He then returned to Lexington to help save Hancock's trunk and papers.

After his exciting midnight ride, Paul continued to help in the patriots' cause. After the war, he went into merchandising and bell casting. During this time, he designed and printed the first Continental money and made the first official seal for the colonies. He retired at age 76 and died of natural causes in May, 1818, at the age of 83. America will never forget this talented artisan and noble patriot!

Color the picture of Paul Revere.

Some of the bells Paul made still ring in New England churches today!

Glossary

artillery: branch of an army that uses large cannons

artisan: a worker who is skilled in a trade; a craftsman

militia: a group of citizens who are not regular soldiers, but who get some military training for service in an emergency

patriot: a person who shows great love and loyalty for his or her country

profession: an occupation for which a person must have a special education or training

Amazing Paul!

Help Paul Revere find his way to warn John Hancock and Samuel Adams that the Redcoats are coming!

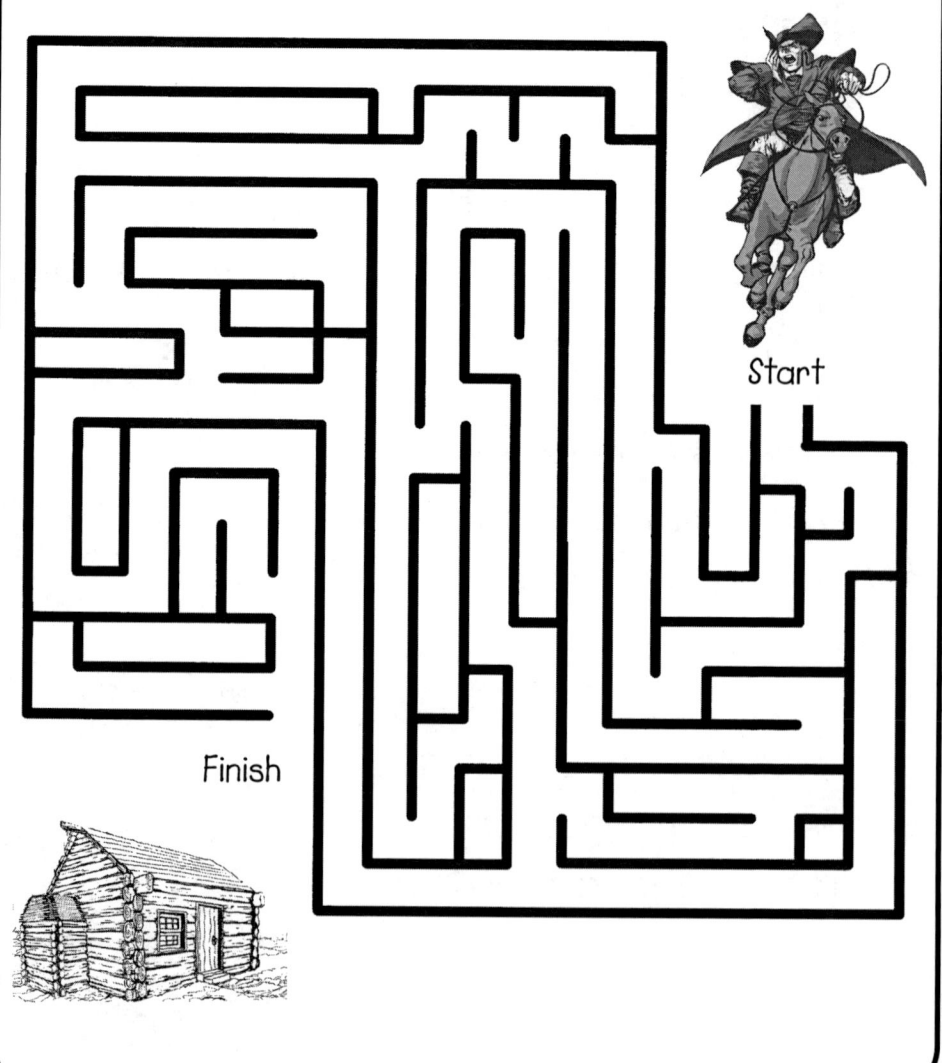

Start

Finish

☙ Pop Quiz! ☙

1. Paul's father's name was originally:
   - ○ Frank
   - ○ George
   - ○ Apollos

2. Paul and his father worked as:
   - ○ silversmiths
   - ○ lawyers
   - ○ teachers

3. People who worked towards the cause of the Revolution were called:
   - ○ patriots
   - ○ thieves
   - ○ miners

4. How many times did Paul marry?
   - ○ 1
   - ○ 2
   - ○ 3

5. Paul was from what Massachusetts city?
   - ○ Pittsburgh
   - ○ Portland
   - ○ Boston

-mendous Trivia!

Whee! I feel like I'm hang-gliding!

Paul Revere's image is on the $5,000 EE Series Savings Bond.

Paul earned extra money ringing the bell at the Old North Church.

Henry Wadsworth Longfellow wrote a poem about Paul's ride.

Do squirrels eat ladybugs?!

Paul Revere was a Freemason.

How many did you get right?